# North Norfolk : coast of contrasts

# North Norfolk : coast of contrasts

Unusual photographs by
## Quentin Quatermain

Avicenna Press
London

First published in 2005 by
Avicenna Press
11 Brownlow Road, London NW10 9QN

Photographs, text and design by Martin Evans,
whose rights have been asserted.

Photographic and graphic processing
by reflections@btconnect.com and sbstudio@hotmail.co.uk
Printed and bound by Kyodo Printing Co (S'pore) Pte Ltd.

ISBN 09547002-1-X

**Cover photograph:** *The* Albatros, *the oldest trading ketch in England, having been built at the turn of the 20th Century. The* Albatros *features strongly in the author's novel* The Rain on My Face, *as the symbol for the sense of freedom felt by those who live on the North Norfolk coast.*
**Half-title page:** "Figures on a North Norfolk beach". *This is a detail from a larger photograph (p 7) the author took of Cley Beach early one January.*
**Facing Title Page:** *This shows the contrast between the beauty yet precise lines of the gable of the author's house and the gentler cluster of the tree's leaves.*
**Facing Contents Page:** *Lobster pots.*
**Facing Introduction:** *Sunset at St Margaret's Church, Cley-next-the-Sea. It is the equinox and the sun is setting in the west – and so it shines straight through the west and east windows. Quentin Quatermain was passing at the time. It has various titles:* "Jonah", "The Devil in Residence" *and* "The Church Crocodile" *among them.*

# Dedication and au revoir

to Prospero, Victor, Zeus
and all my friends in North Norfolk
with love

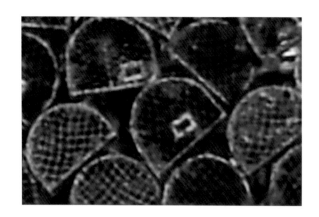

# CONTENTS

Introduction

9

Winter - Dawn

1

Spring - Morning

21

Summer - Afternoon

53

Autumn - Evening

99

# INTRODUCTION

Some of the photographs in this book were carefully prepared – and some were snap shots. It's difficult to tell the difference. Some subjects were never photographed before even though they are beautiful and even though thousands of people have seen many of them many times. And some were never seen before. It's difficult to tell the difference. Some were taken with expensive cameras; some with much cheaper cameras. Footnotes show when I used a Mamiya 6 x 4 with 55mm, 30-90mm and 70-210mm lenses, a £10 Kodak camera or a disposable camera. If not shown, I used a Pentax Z 70 with 55mm and 70-210mm lenses. But it's difficult to tell the difference.

All you need is the eye.

So what is a good photograph? You might as well ask: "What is a good painting?" Is it what fancy art critics call "the quintessence of the subject"? Maybe they mean "the heart of the matter" (The Catholic Times), or "what makes it tick" (The Sun). But quintessence is subjective and varies with the times. That's why Van Gogh died never having sold a picture and why a Japanese bank later bought his 'Sunflowers' for $30 million and buried it in a bank vault. And it's why popular artists suit the times and why we think an unmade bed is not a vain and ludicrous joke but worth buying.

This is a personal selection of subjects near Cley-next-the-Sea. Anyone could have filled a dozen books with different photographs. But although many subjects are here – little-known but beautiful houses, reeds, doors in Wells, fishermen – two things stand out: contrast and pattern. Contrast is strong in North Norfolk. See wave-marked mud in a creek next to a clump of reed stalks and you see two contrasting patterns, each strengthening the other. Intensity – that's life! Pattern is something you can find everywhere – boles in tree trunks, flint walls, reeds, shadows, doors, crabs, leaves, furrows, snow crystals on hay, tractor marks. Not just that. Pattern, which you find in detail, is man's greatest need. It helps us find a reason for our existence. By concentrating on them this book tries to show how pattern, detail and contrast are everywhere. Finding it creates harmony, fulfilment and beauty. Knowing that, we can at least die happy.

One problem photographers share with painters is to turn two dimensions into three. So I often use an object in the foreground with lines into the picture to give depth and lead the eye to something at the back. But another problem that painters had was the invention of photography in the 1850s. Apart from its versatility, how could they compete with someone who could depict a scene in a second or two that took them three months to paint? So they sneered at it – and still do. Not long ago Matisse said that photography would be best known for recording their work. Much earlier (in 1863) a few others just took their spectacles off and, after an appropriate purgatory in the Salon des Refusés, became the Impressionists. And if today a photographer took a blurred picture of a few haystacks his picture will be sneered at – unlike Monet's!

I start the book with an example of North Norfolk's painful winter beauty. This bare tree near Susted is being strangled and its black branches are scrabbling at the sky. Land and road are black too – also flat. Even the puddle is flat. The road leads to a flat horizon and more strangled trees. It's not pretty but it has great beauty. And it's The Edge!

The dawn comes up like thunder in North Norfolk – if you get up early enough. I shot this from the landing window of my house in Cley-next-the-Sea and then went back to bed. The birds were scattering like grapeshot.

# Winter ~ Dawn

Snow crystals radiate around stalks of hay on the ground. This shot taken near Warham demonstrates the beauty and pattern in detail. It's all there. All you need do is look closely enough. And by going in close you can exclude distraction.

The churchyard at St Nicholas Church in Wells-next-the-Sea. I got up early for this picture, too. I was shooting straight into the sun but the trees hid the light and the tombstones' shadows gave depth. While I was there the heavens opened, a shower of manna came down and a drop baptized the lens.

Binham Priory was founded in 1091 by Peter de Valoines, a nephew of William the Conqueror. Various priors sold the silver, wasted money on lawyers, used forged deeds, behaved objurgatorily, fled owing £600, became vagabonds and caused a local prior to be flogged before burial in chains: none of which are considered orthodox Christian policy. The railings lead your gaze to the Priory and their end pillar gives depth.

Norfolk has Britain's most varied larder – these are some of the fish caught off its coast. I shot the fish in a shop in Cley and deliberately overflowed the edges of the picture to give a feeling of abundance.

Snow seems to emphasise North Norfolk's harsh landscape. Even the gable of my house seems to stick up from the snow like a thumb – admittedly a pretty thumb. A straightforward shot, although it's as well to open the exposure a little to keep the snow white.

The first week in January, and too cold on the beach at Cley for only a few minutes but I saw this fisherman suddenly run down and cast his line. The scene was grainy, pointilliste, like a Seurat. I hadn't noticed the group of four figures in the distance, but they became the picture on the half-title page. Probably the easiest and most profitable picture I ever took – and often mistaken for a painting (as if that were a compliment).

Ice in tractor marks near Langham airfield. A simple shot but showing a pattern – another aspect of beauty, since patterns show harmony, a quality of beauty. And all you need do is look for it.

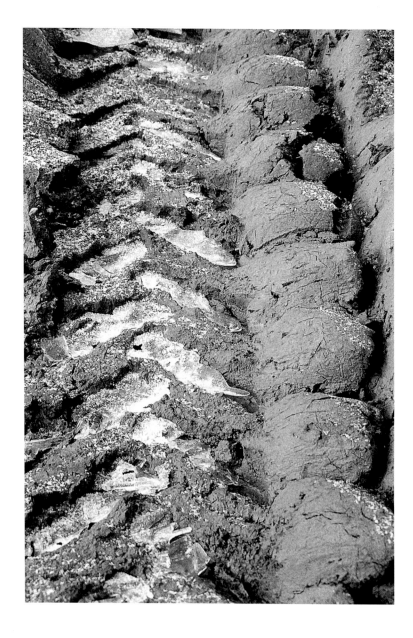

St Margaret's Church, Cley. I took this Christmas Card shot during a weekend wander down to the Three Swallows pub. The bushes give depth and the pub bench gives contrast. I've no idea what the exposure was. Actually, I think the camera had only one speed, though I never looked. But to be safe I took the picture before I went in to the pub. *A £10 Kodak camera.*

Old Womans Lane at Cley. A shot where the road gives depth and direction as it runs from the camera into the distance. You can't avoid following it.

Morston Church – another example of lines deepening a picture, this time snow on the furrows. And a view of this church probably never taken before under snow. *Fuji S 5000 digital.*

This could be anything from an aerial view of the next ice age, an electron micro-photograph of a particularly virulent disease (avian 'flu?), a company of advancing Soviet troops disguised in their winter camouflage (snow on their boots, too), a penicillin mould on marmalade or even rough grass at Stody covered by snow. Whichever it is, there's always a pattern that's not there by accident.

Under snow: the gamekeeper's cottage on the road to Holt. A pretty shot, even cosy – unlike many of houses under snow. Again the road and the snow-outlined furrows give depth and the cottage provides the focus. And beyond the cottage the way the road curves round the woods and vanishes makes you wonder what might be appearing next.

*Left:* A very odd landscape between Wells-next-the-Sea and Binham – another one that has probably never been photographed before. The snow contrasts with the woodland and makes the picture unusually geometric, like a chequerboard. An example of patterns in a landscape. But come the Spring and all will change.

A lane leading off the road from Holt to the coast. Again I used the lane to deepen the picture and the tree on the left to balance the lane's turnings. *Overleaf:* another early morning shot, this time between Wighton and Langham. I was gazing mesmerised at the trees being strangled beneath that cumulo-nimbus sky when a cyclist shot past me and I used him as a focus for the road's lead-in. *A £10 Kodak camera.*

*Previous page:* it's probably impossible to produce a book of photographs of North Norfolk without showing Cley windmill. Here the snow makes it seem an outpost – and the River Glaven leads the eye towards it. The sea is half a mile across the marshes behind the camera.

A medieval scene outside Cley: near-black and made more inhospitable by the cold snow outlining the ploughed furrows leading to the silhouette of St Margaret's Church that seems to oversee it all. An unwelcoming and even insecure atmosphere. Totally unlike my picture of the same church on p9, but shot only a week later. *A 20-yr-old Mamiya 6 x 4, 70-135mm zoom lens.*

*Opposite:* The night fishing's over. It's shortly after dawn and three lads have caught the tide so there's water over the bar on the River Glaven. They're homeward bound through the marshes to Cley with a full catch – and beds waiting.

Budding thistle in my garden, often a false spring in North Norfolk. Shooting with light behind a subject almost gives it the quality of a hologram.

The tree is in fresh blossom over this Cley cottage wall and the yellow wallflowers are out. It looks at last like Easter – but is it? For this is North Norfolk, home of false alarms.

# Spring ~ Morning

Wiveton Hall. One of North Norfolk's most unknown yet most beautiful and romantic mansions, its site worthy of a Daphne du Maurier novel at the marsh's edge … hidden by tall trees … down a rutted drive … two ancient gables … its farm producing pheasants and pigs, strawberries and spinach … high walls protect a kitchen garden from the north wind … seat of a distinguished family. A Spring day and the daffodils are out.

This looks like summer but I took it in March for an April exhibition. I used a technique to make it seem hazy and several lines (two walls, the road and two verges) to draw the eye to the lady with the red parasol. An American photographer I once worked for said: "Always use some red, it's a photographer's favourite colour". The abstract blaze to the right makes it very summer-like. Someone who had thought it was a painting said: "It could almost be a photograph." Was that a compliment?

This mere near an ornithologist's hide outside Salthouse was taken in very early Spring. Everything is still a bit chilly.

But using flash with a close-up of some of the reeds silhouetted against the black woods behind makes the picture more striking and unusual. Perhaps even Spring-like. *Mamiya 6 x 4, 55m lens.*

The east window of
St Margaret's Church,
Saxlingham. The wording
above is: "Behold a sower
went forth to sow." The
inscriptions are (left to
right): "I am the true vine",
"He spake many things to
them in parables", and
"I am the bread of life."
The church is mentioned in
the Domesday Book. Records
date from 1558 – the year of
accession of England's greatest
monarch, who defended it
against the Pope, Spain and
half Europe and guided
it in "the spacious days"
to political, literary and
maritime magnificence.

Salthouse Marsh, beyond the
rise lies the sea. One's eye
automatically follows a line
of posts linked by wires that
recedes into the distance.
It's useful to show
perspective – even when
it doesn't lead anywhere.
More – this line divides a
pool, each side of which
appears identical. But then
border disputes seem to be
the county sport, if not art
form, of North Norfolk.

I've always been fascinated by scrap yards. You have to be an Autolycus, a picker-up of unconsidered trifles, for you never know what you might find. Long ago I found a Rolls-Royce in one. But here in Holt there's a huge contrast between the yard and the trim bungalow next to it, in which resides the owner. But this is North Norfolk.
*Fuji S 5000 digital.*

Also by contrast, not more than a few miles away outside Baconsthorpe is this grand and classic gem – and it's a farmhouse. As Cobbett pointed out – "You find the grandest houses where the land is best." Yes, this is North Norfolk.
*Fuji S 5000 digital.*

28

Intricacies and beauty
of detail usually go
unnoticed unless you cut
out surrounding features.
Wood's knobs and growth
rings can give much
pleasure as objets trouvés
and often inspiration.
From a tree in a wood
outside Thornage.

An unusual picture of
Cley from the road from
Blakeney at the entrance to
Wiveton Hall. It's not often
that you can show Cley
village, the Mill, the marshes
and the sea in one picture –
unless you're in a plane.
But then it loses its
human scale.

Knapped flints – part of a house near a ford outside Letheringset. Their chequerboard appearance is pleasing and such flints usually appear on important buildings such as churches. *A £10 Kodak camera.*

Bloaters being smoked and hanging in the Smokehouse at Cley. This is the only place I know where you can buy them. Their extra flavour comes because they aren't split open like kippers before they're being smoked. Flash essential.

I found fascinating that every time the track dipped and rose its white and dark lines alternated – but I was standing in the position to see it. Three feet to the left or right – and they didn't alternate. But the track would still lead the eye into the picture. Near the little-used hill road from Holt to Cley.

Just a post in the marsh … yes, but it's another example of finding something interesting when you discover its detail: it almost looks like an Aboriginal pattern. Such things are everywhere, are usually taken for granted but nearly always can give inspiration. Blakeney Marsh.
*Disposable camera.*

Although the prevalent wind is from the south west (luckily – otherwise we'd all be flooded every year) the north wind is strong enough to blow the coastal trees southwards. The tracks lead the eye towards them, as usual. Next to the coast road between Weybourne and Sheringham.

A pattern of flint and brick. They are always fascinating because they're all different. The bricks seem to be finding it difficult to get into line. But easy to photograph – so long as you see it. Cley Mill. *A £10 Kodak camera.*

A Loke in Cley – alley ways
linking the roads and wide
enough for a smuggler.
There are plenty of
wallflowers and some tulips.
The hollyhocks will soon
appear. I had to wait for
a van at the end to drive
off and reveal the blue
door. While I waited I
photographed the Loke
when a man stood for a
moment at the end. Then
I cut him out from the print,
stuck him into the picture
with the blue door and
printed the result.

Even agricultural machinery
has poetry and pattern.
A passing shot near a farm
outside Edgefield. It has
intentional function and
unintentional mystery.

The enigmatic Belgian painter Magritte lives yet; this time in Salthouse. As soon as you can see that the round windows are startled eyes and notice the quiff of hair and the ridge of an adenoidal nose – you can't get rid of any of it. Looks like a Tory politician. *Fuji S 5000 digital.*

A really beautiful composition – and all natural. A bush in the foreground. Furrows leading in a sensitive curve to focus at a lone bush on the horizon. I stopped the car and shot it – an instant snap. I went back the next day because the light was a little better. But the farmer had already ploughed it over and the pattern had vanished. At the coast road between Weybourne and Sheringham.

More flint and bricks.
I could photograph a
couple of dozen flint and
brick walls and never get
anywhere near duplicating
them. Vive la difference.
This one was in my
garden in Cley.
*A disposable camera.*

This contrasting picture
shows how tree branches
grow to an optimum length
for their needs, approaching
the arc of a circle. This most
satisfying shape of all is the
simplest pattern in nature.
It also presents a dilemma
about the meaning of life –
which of course leads to
replication. The high road
between Holt and Cley.

Kippers – the breakfast
food that lasts all day.
Flash essential.
Cley Smokehouse.

This is how they make
barn windows in North
Norfolk – a fascinating
example of creating beauty
out of function and the
harmony of a pattern.
Ruskin was right after all.
A barn near Stody.
*A £10 Kodak camera.*

The source of the River Glaven, somewhere near Holt. Again I used a technique to get this picture, which looks as if the early morning mist was still around. It wasn't.

One of the many fields in North Norfolk filled by poppies in summer. *A £10 Kodak camera.*

When in the 1890s a London journalist took the train to Cromer for a weekend he became highly enthusiastic about North Norfolk (perhaps mildly influenced by a miller's beautiful daughter), named the area Poppyland and wrote a lot of sentimental Victorian poetry about it.

A large and homely vase filled with honesty plants, props open the front door of my house and filters in the sunlight. These are last year's plants, but they aren't called "everlastings" for nothing. Although the heart-shaped toothed leaves have fallen, light still shines through the shiny disc that holds the seeds.

A simple example of contrasts, so simple that no-one gives it a second thought. Yet it has harmony. Moreover the ripples could be water or could be mud. But they are definitely have the outline of electro-magnetic waves of which, incidentally, the whole universe consists.
Blakeney Creek.
*A £10 Kodak camera.*

High flung clouds fill the
sky while the church at
Corpusty huddles far below.

All the lights in my house
seem to be on. The sky has
taken on a soft and velvet
texture. Is Summer really
about to arrive? This
picture was subject to heavy
manipulation to stop the
lights spreading out of the
windows. I superimposed
two pictures on one –
and printed the result.

A row of trees on the skyline near Edgefield. The weather is dark and threatening.

A few minutes later. Now the sun has reappeared and the scene is completely different – more promise for the summer. A typical example of North Norfolk's sudden change of weather.

# Summer ~ Afternoon

A happy English Summer
scene – and a corner of
my garden. I paid £1 for
the roller and 50p for the
watering can at Aylsham's
Monday auction. That
makes me feel happier.
*Fuji S 5000 digital.*

Another sign that
Summer's here. Someone
has launched his boat
and gone for a picnic
on the marshes. You can
see Blakeney Church on
the horizon; the sea is
behind the camera and
Blakeney Point is out of
sight to the right.

Cley Mill, a novel view.
The mill used to grind
wheat for loading on ships
when the estuary silted up.
Now it's a bed & breakfast
and a subject for trendy
photographs.
*Mamiya 6 x 4, 55mm lens.*

Cley Old Hall, one of
the oldest buildings in
the village, shot from
the top of the mill.
*Mamiya 6 x 4, 55mm lens.*

Cley Beach and an
interesting occupation
for a couple in their Third
Age, an improvement on
two deck chairs at Torquay.
*Fuji S 5000 digital.*

I swung the camera around
to the right to show the
pill box. That and all the
rest gave them the life, and
the freedom, to sit there.
Many pill boxes, long since
dilapidated still stand in
North Norfolk, at road
junctions or on high
ground. Each one was more
important than the Tower of
London. And then there are
the small buildings, ruined
now but still with wire masts
sticking out of their roofs
and always near flat ground
with wide concrete roadways
always pointing south-west
to north-east. Now no
longer enough to keep
Europe out.

Another example of how detail can usually go unnoticed. Wood's knobs and growth rings can give a great deal of pleasure as obje's trouvés and often inspiration. Surprisingly this is even greater when shot in close-up and enlarged. Found in a wood near Stiffkey.

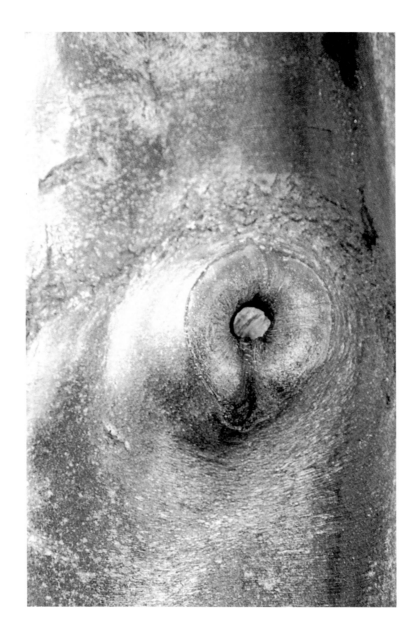

Blakeney Regatta: sailing in a sea mist – or is it? It looks a foggy day but I shot in bright sunlight. So how did it get like this? Yes, it was the technique! But also I had to compose the picture – wait until the yacht was sailing towards the sun's reflection, focus the camera, vary the zoom, give orders to the helmsman, keep the horizon horizontal while my dinghy was rolling and pitching – and prepare for that technique. I took 20 or 30 shots to get this picture. Hard work, oh yes!

Just a bit of marsh? Yes.
But seek and you will find
… the shadows are more
beautiful than the substance
– an example of Plato's
shadows made by something
inside a cave that you can't
see but is nothing like the
shadows. In fact we think
the shadow is the reality.
Not just a bit of sedge,
even on Blakeney Creek.

A thoroughly unchristian-
looking eagle posing as a
lectern in Saxlingham
Church. I had to stand
precariously on the tops
of two pews to take this.
*Fuij S 5000 digital.*

Crabs: good enough to
eat – or to use for a
wallpaper pattern.

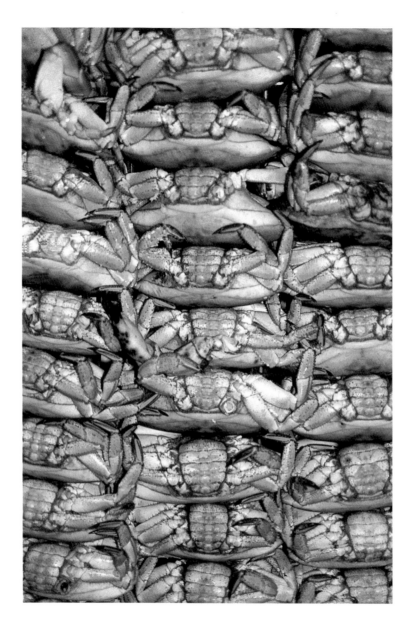

This avenue of trees leads to
another of the grand houses
hidden away in this old
county – Little Barningham
Hall at Matlaske. In the
18thC the Winter family
sold it to Edward Paston,
who then went bankrupt.
The Mott family bought
it in 1785, married into the
Radclyffe family and they've
all been there together ever
since, give or take a war or
two with the Germans, which
depleted the family's stock
if not their pluck.

*Page 66 overleaf:* a close-up
picture of the same Hall.
*Fuji S 5000 digital, 10x zoom.*

Another simple picture on Blakeney Creek that, apart from Ophelia, could attract several interpretations – green hair, a river's delta, molten traces on a newly discovered planet or, upside down, green fire. Or just an interesting organic pattern.

The next four pages show photographs of houses, doors, little corners and the odd boat or two at Wells. Very easy to take (I just walked round Wells for a hour or two) and producing a fascinating contrast.

  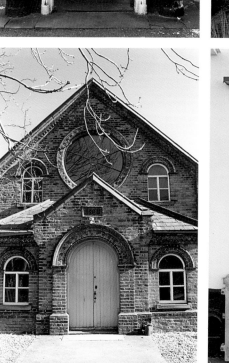 

The rounded top tiles of this flint wall in Cley encourages rainwater to bounce off each side and miss the wall. Below them, the flat tiles project outwards for the same reason. Next comes a row of bricks, often more resilent to rain than the mortar betwen the flints.

Haddock in Cley Smokehouse. Flash essential. A surrealist, even revolutionary, pattern worthy of Dali and Buneal's "Le Chien Andalou."

North Norfolk, not
Provence. The elderberry:
in spring, a white blossom
to make a sparkling white
wine. Now swells the juicy
purple berries to make rich
ruby red wine in September,
ready for Xmas. And
all begun outside my
bathroom window.
*A £10 Kodak camera.*

Hollyhocks and hibiscus in
full bloom in my garden.

A fisherman casts his line into the sea off Weybourne. I used an anchor and various lobster pots in the foreground to give depth and a bit of relief from the beach's monotony. *Fuji S 5000 digital.*

In the 1970s I could have bought this barn (with planning permission) in Wighton for £1,000. This one is still there, and so are the poppies and wallflowers, which turn it into a thing of beauty – once you look.

I found this lobster pot on a beach somewhere. It had been battered by a storm, so I stuck it on a wall. Well, better than a garden gnome. It seems to have a strong attraction for ivy, which I have to cut away at least once a month.
*Fuji S 5000 digital.*

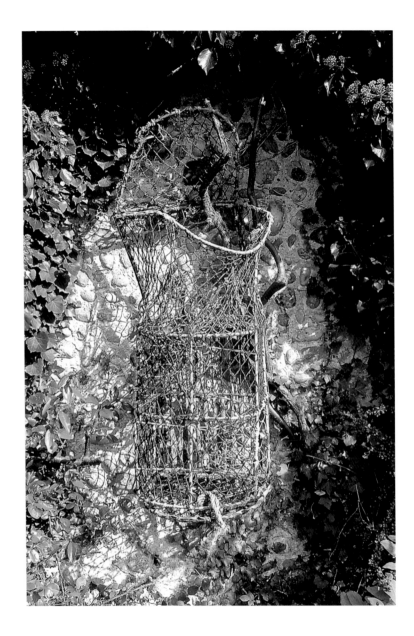

Outside Letheringset. There's something irresistible about a cottage with an open bedroom window in late afternoon. The clear sky, the shadows across the lane, the hazy air into which the lane gently disappears and the generous welcome hinted at by the open window – they all symbolize peace and contentment. I came, I saw, I snapped – and walked on.
*A £10 Kodak camera.*

A golden summer evening on the River Glaven near the road between Cley and Holt. Reeds line the right bank like a ruffled sleeve. The nearest reeds glow brightly and add depth. The river leads the eye back to Wiveton Church on the horizon. Several thousand people must pass that spot every day. But how many look at it?

*Pages 81-85*. Huge numbers of reeds grow on the North Norfolk coastline, particularly its marshes. Its growing, harvesting and marketing, largely for thatching roofs, is a significant and very long-established local industry. The following five pages illustrate part of its harvesting and stacking near Salthouse and at the Glaven's sluicegate in Cley.

The reed (Phragmites communis) is a large perennial herb of the natural order Gramineae. It is a native of Europe, Asia, Africa, America and Australia, growing on the margins of lakes, streams, and up wet sea-cliffs.

The reed is a very erect growth, the stout, round stems reaching 10-15ft, with broad flat rigid leaves. The flowers are gathered in a large, oval, purplish plume.

Reeds are the predominant plant in the fens of East Anglia and in the floating fens found at the mouths of the Danube and in the Black Sea.

When stacked the bundles of reeds take on the pattern of a hexagonal section. You can see it here at the end of a stack.

This shows the bundle of reeds in some detail, now demonstrating their hollow nature. The pattern is more detailed than the hexagon. This enlargement is not great: the greater your enlargement the more pattern you can see in its composition.

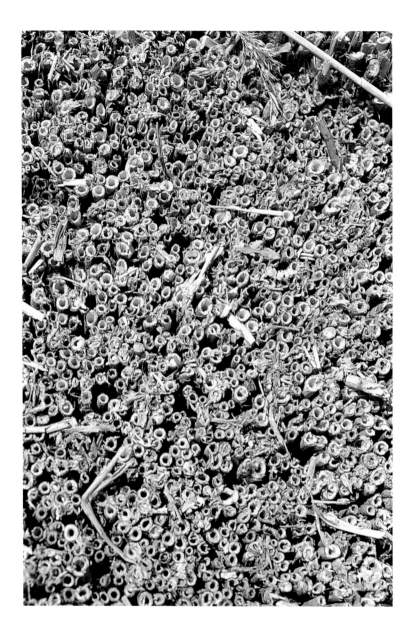

Like all organic matter reeds can be beautiful. The following page shows an elegant, almost Pre-Raphaelite, pattern at the ends of a stack. But it's functional. The small horizontal bundles are stuffed between the rows of larger bundles to stop the rain seeping inwards. And gravity adds a wan and melancholic elegance to the plumes – which become a neglected Rossetti model.

Blakeney Creek. This picture shows the delicate essence of the plant revealed by its shadow – together with the contrast between the animus, the shadow's elegant feminine nature and the anima, the uncompromising hard and masculine post with its unsubtle shadow stretching commandingly out of the picture. Or maybe it's just a nice picture.
*A disposable camera.*

This is inside a barn near Baconsthorpe and I still am not certain what it's a picture of. The bayonet knife is menacing the white sack that seems to have its hands up. But what's inside it? Will it bleed grain – or deflate? Is this a Ku Klux Klan meeting interrupted by a gang of corn-fed assassins? Or is it the sudden discovery of a disguised interloper, a spy infiltrating a secret meeting of Norfolk insurgents? No one knows.
*Fuji S 5000 digital.*

Another picture of a detail –
this time of wormholes in
a dead tree trunk between
Holt and Edgecomb.
Again, a close-up isolates
them from nearby
distractions and discloses
their pattern and contrast
with the actual wood.

Various doors to houses
in Cley. Showing only
the doors without their
surrounds makes you
concentrate on them
and demonstrates their
variety and fascination.
This time I walked round
for less than an hour.

Holkham Beach. This buoy is neither flotsam nor jetsam and anyway vanished two days later. The picture gives an easily grasped idea of foreground and depth (the knot in the rope), something to guide the eye to the subject (the rope) and the subject (the buoy) more or less placed at a text-book position at the top right.

Stacked and empty lobster pots fill the fishing boat on Cley beach. The fishermen began stacking the pots by carefully laying them out in a neat row on the ground. In the next row they fitted the edges of the pots between those in the first row. They made an effort to do the same for the third and fourth rows but in the end got fed up, threw them on the stack just to get rid of them and went off to the pub.
*Fuji S 5000 digital.*

There's nothing particularly
odd about this picture.
It's natural to stick a big
fork into some bales of hay.
But maybe that's why I took
it. The pattern or symbolism
in natural things is often
ignored. For example,
those bales are obviously
dead and the fork killed
them all: Bosworth Field
all over again.
*Mamiya 6 x 4, 55 mm lens.*

Weybourne Beach – and a
fishing boat is loaded with
piles of coiled ropes, nets,
oars, plastic containers,
tyres, buoys and pennants.
Fishing's clearly over
for the day.
*A disposable camera.*

*Pages 94 and 95:*
Cley Allotments.
Again the fascination
of photographing details
and of their contrast
seen together.

Near Cley Mill. Walls are often built with flint and brick mixed together, but not often with such an intriguing brick pattern. A minor example of using detail but also showing contrast, since the bricks are set in a more orderly way than the flints.
*A £10 Kodak camera.*

Winter feed near Corpusty: it keeps green inside the black bags but slowly becomes sweaty. I spent an afternoon driving round North Norfolk photographing sileage bales. This was the ambiguous one – barrels of armagnac or a herd of sleeping hippos? And the tractor was in the classic position. Final bonus – rays from a low sun reflected off a few bales and gave them a bit of diversity.

Leaves fall around this 18thC mileage post. Autumn has arrived. I was on the way home from the weekly auction at Aylsham, having bought a Flymo. It was after I'd taken this picture that I discovered it didn't work. So I painted it another colour and put it back in the sale the following week.

Cley. A cool clear sky to the east, long shadows, an empty beach and a fishing boat safely anchored for winter. They conclude that Summer is indeed over – pieced together as if from clues in a murder mystery.

# Autumn ~ Evening

Between Cley and Blakeney.
The gate swings ajar as the
boys throw their bikes on
the lawn, dash in through
the front door and scramble
onto their chairs for potted
shrimps, tea and bed later.
They must make the most
of their last supper, for
holidays are over. I worked
all this out in the moment
it took to walk past.
A text-book impulse shot
where you shoot first
and ask afterwards. Also
text-book Cartier-Bresson.
*A £10 Kodak camera.*

The sun shines warmly on
the rusted old anchor at
Weybourne Beach but its
glow is cool and the shadows
long. The tide's out and the
anchor is beached, if not
swallowed. Anchor and day
are both in decline. Rather
like a fish hook and too big
for an objet-trouvé, it has a
subtle colour variety and,
more important, has no
doubt saved a few ships.
A low camera angle shows
some background as well.

Autumn has stripped bare the trees of this wood near Aylsham and the ruts are already rich with the mulch of rotted leaves. A lone dog bursts across the track after a rabbit.

Again it's worth looking closely at mundane things. And again the shadow doesn't match up to the reality. The short straggles of dry seaweed on this rope at Morston Creek could be from Conan Doyle's "The Dancing Men" or a Karaghiosis shadow play, but definitely too good for the Tate Modern, let alone the Royal Academy. *A £10 Kodak camera.*

A last burst of autumn
sunlight on Blakeney Creek
and a rich healthy colour
of the marram grass.
Glistening like the skin
of a new-born animal, that
shining gunmetal mud looks
so beautiful. You wouldn't
think it could be dangerous.

There's not much in this
picture of the River Glaven
below Cley. A wide and
empty sky. The tide is
low and a lone yacht sits
stranded on the mud. Only
two people around – and far
off at that. A lot of scrubby
grass and no sun. But that's
the point. That's what the
marshes are like when
autumn sets in. Not all
sunny and picture-book
like the page opposite.

Cley harbour, the River
Glaven, the marshes and
Blakeney Church, all from
the top of Cley Mill. The
river's on the ebb. Soon
the tide will be coming in.
*Mamiya 6 x 4,*
*210mm zoom lens.*

Near Blakeney Point.
A rich sunset and a golden
sky. Result: contentment.

*Overleaf, p108:* in two
minutes the scene has
completely changed:
no sun, grey sky, grey water.
Result: gloom. Typical
of North Norfolk's quick
weather change. *p109:* the
tide hurries in at Blakeney
Creek. *p110:* Blakeney
Marsh, light fades.
*p111:* Birds rise over an
abandoned dinghy. *p112:*
the birds have gone and
now fog creeps in over
the boat. *p113:* Wiveton
Church, near sunset.
*Mamiya 6x4,*
*190mm zoom lens.*

Landfall. The straggler at Blakeney Regatta is nearly home at last. Booby prize: now there's enough water to tie up at the quay.

Sunset and tide approach on the River Glaven. Now floats the lone yacht.

Cley High St. The dying sun reflected from high strato-cumulus clouds gave such a dramatic sunset that also contrasted with the buildings that I took my camera out into the street. While I was there a sinister pair of headlights broke up the dark and made the contrast more dynamic. *A £10 Kodak camera.*

Blakeney Church at sunset from a path leading down to Cley Allotments. I saw the sunset from my garden and rushed up to take the shot. I needed a tripod for such a time of day and took several shots. I printed this exposure because in it a last ray has shot rather desperately out of the clouds as if the sun had changed its mind about setting.

A rare shot of the mill from a spot as high as its first floor yet silhouetted against an empty sky. A tripod gave me a long exposure and a long telephone lens got me close up and I could even crop the picture – which makes you feel even closer.
*Mamiya 6 x 4,*
*210mm zoom lens.*

The end of the day on Blakeney Creek. I'd have looked a bit weird walking around the creek with a tripod, so I rested the camera on a post for the long exposure needed. *p120:* A more ordinary sort of photograph of Cley Mill compared with the one on p118, but with the most superb sunset imagineable and the first I ever took of the Mill. *p121:* This is how Cley mashes really look in winter. Not comfortable. In fact a late work by the celebrated 17thC Dutch landscape artist, van der Meurve.
*A £10 Kodak camera, image printed from a laser copy, the grain of which becomes fog.*
*p122:* Trudging home at Cley Beach. *p123:* Four trees in fog near Wareham.

I came upon these two boats while wandering down the River Glaven in a winter's late-afternoon fog. Close up, they were easy to see. *Fuji S 5000 digital.*

But 50 yards further on I looked back and already they were almost out of sight. *Fuji S 5000 digital.*

The lone sailor nearing journey's end at Cley Mill. Now no birds sing and only the outboard motor's soft beat breaks the marshland's silence. The sailor's cut-out silhouette imposes attention. The high sky and the monotone of the clouds increase the feeling of his isolation.
*A £10 Kodak camera.*

That evening the sailor and I hung three woodcock over my dining room fire and set slices of bread below each one. In five minutes they were ready.

*p128:* Cley Church: *Mamiya 6 x 4, 55mm lens, 10 min existing light exposure, with flash at the altar. p129:* Cley Church Tower in a crown of thorns. *p130:* Freak shaft of sunlight near Cley. *p131:* Binham Priory.